I0424672

CONTENTS

INTRODUCTION

This book is not about teaching you something or about biographies. I've noticed my environment, friends and colleagues talking and discussing (a.k.a gossiping) about people they have never actually met and probably will never meet in their entire life. People like the latest celebrity, reality contestant, singer, actor, and any other celebrity appearing on every magazine/website.

That's when I started thinking that in the span of humanity, there have been countless gossip-worthy facts in the life of people who are worth-knowing who we don't know. We just keep busy with the latest gossip that happened. I went on a journey to find out about the facts in the lives of people worth-knowing who are either alive or who have lived in previous centuries.

Just to be clear, some of the people that follow are controversial figures. They are not necessarily worthy people, rather than being worth knowing about. I tend to focus on a single event in the life of these people that might be gossiped about if happened today. If you find something interesting, I would urge you to just pull out that phone in your pocket and Google the person. You would be surprised by how interesting the life of people who have lived in previous centuries has been (without implying that our life is not interesting :).

PETER THE GREAT

Peter the Great was the ruler of the Russian Empire from 1682 to 1725. Peter was no ordinary leader. He is the one who actually created the Russian Empire; before him, it was called the Tsardom of Russia and it was significantly smaller.

What is really interesting about Peter is that before starting his big reforms in the country, he made a long trip to Europe. This trip was no conventional trip though. It was dubbed the "Grand Embassy" and aimed to visit European leaders to build alliances for facing the Ottoman Empire in the future.

For the entire duration of this long trip (it lasted 18 months!), he traveled incognito with a fake identity (!), even though he was the most powerful man of Russia. He did this mainly to allow him to avoid any social and diplomatic obligations. The real question is whether he fooled anybody since he was significantly taller than most of his contemporaries. He was quite tall even for modern times; he stood 2.03m (6 ft 8) in height, so he was literally at least a head above an average person in Russia and Europe.

Peter returned from his trip with the perception that European customs were superior to the Russian ones. He gave an order for all of his officials to wear European clothes and to cut their long beards. Of course, he was no dictator. Whoever wanted to keep his beard could do so by paying a crazy amount of money called a "beard tax."

CLINT EASTWOOD

Y ou may know Clint from his movies (or even his music, yes he is a musician too) but if you haven't paid attention to his family life you are in for a surprise. It's well known that Clint was married and divorced multiple times. What not many people know is that he has a daughter, called Laurie, who he didn't even know about.

Keeping the long story short, it seems Clint had a relationship with Laurie's mother in Seattle before becoming a star. Their relationship ended, but the woman, who is not yet publicly identified, was pregnant and had their baby. This is where things get weird. She did not contact Clint at all and gave the baby for adoption.

The baby, a now 60-something-year-old mother of two called Laurie, was adopted by a family in Seattle. When she grew up, around 30 years ago, she decided to search for her biological parents, and found out about her real biological father. It appears Clint had no idea Laurie's mother was pregnant, but he received the news positively and kept a close relationship with her ever since. He appeared at the Oscars with her, attended his granddaughter's marriage and they spent Thanksgiving together a few times.

Laurie is not an actor (or a musician), but they both share a love for golf and spending free time outside. The story is entirely true, although it could easily be a movie script with a happy ending and probably be quite successful!

At the time of writing, Clint was 88 years old and still actively working on movies (directing mainly). We can 'blame' his extremely good physical condition on the conscious healthy lifestyle and eating habits he has adopted since he was a teenager (!) and his daily meditation.

THEODORE ROOSEVELT

Theodore was one of the most influential presidents of the United States. His face is even on Mount Rushmore (if you don't know it already, you've probably seen it; it's the heads of four great American presidents carved into the granite face of a mountain). But I am not here to talk about politics or the reforms Theodore was responsible for, but rather about how he miraculously survived an assassination attempt.

While he was heading to give a speech for his campaign somewhere in Wisconsin, a guy named John Flammang Schrank shot him once in the chest. The bullet went through his steel eyeglass case and the single-folded 50-page copy of his speech and hit him in the chest. The assassin was immediately disarmed. The crowd gathered to listen to Theodore was ready to lynch Schrank when they heard Theodore shouting and demanding that the suspect was to remain unharmed. Police took the suspect into custody and Theodore assured the crowd he was fine. With blood on his shirt (!), he completed his scheduled speech, and only after 90 minutes did he accept medical help.

Roosevelt was an experienced hunter and anatomist and he figured out the bullet had not reached his lung since he was not coughing blood. That's why he decided to go on with his speech. Indeed, x-ray screenings afterward showed the bullet had hit his chest muscle, but stopped there and didn't penetrate any further. The doctors actually concluded it would be more dangerous to try to remove the bullet. In the end, Theodore had the bullet in his chest for the rest of his life!

ALBERT EINSTEIN

I don't think Albert needs any introduction. His name is synonymous with genius and he is maybe the most important scientist of the last century. And for a good reason; his contributions to physics changed the way people understood (and still understand) space, time, mass, and energy. The stereotypical personal life of a scientist is to be quiet and not very interesting. What is not widely known is that Albert's personal life was not quiet nor usual at all.

His first known crash was with his professor's daughter at secondary school. Her name was Marie. Not much is known about this relationship. His first serious relationship was with Mileva Marić, who was also enrolled at Zurich Polytechnic where Albert was studying. It is suspected, due to an early correspondence that was discovered and published years later, that the couple had a daughter born in Serbia (Mileva was from there).

Unfortunately, the child did not survive due to scarlet fever or it was given up for adoption. The real name and the fate of the baby are still unknown to this day. After this incident, Albert and Mileva got married and had 2 sons Hans and Edward while living in Switzerland.

In letters discovered recently, it appears Albert was writing love letters to his first love, Marie while his wife was pregnant with their second child. A few years after the birth of their second son, the couple separated after Mileva learned about Albert's secret affair with his ..... first and second cousin Elsa. She was a first cousin from his mother's side and a second cousin from his father's side. Finally, Albert married Elsa and moved to the U.S.A. a few years after his official divorce.

CHARLIE CHAPLIN

C harlie was one of the greatest and most widely known public figures of his time. The younger generation might know him only as a classic figure who made some legendary films during the era of the silent cinema, but he did way more than just that and his career spanned more than 75 years. He had a very tough childhood in London, where he was born and grew up. His father was constantly absent and his mother was struggling financially and was committed to a mental asylum when he was 14. Overall, Charlie had an amazingly interesting life that couldn't fit into this short space here. I urge you to look him up!

One of the weirdest events of Charlie's life though was during the mid-1940s. It seems a young actress named Joan Barry had an on-and-off affair with him during 1941-1942, but they eventually separated. Joan showed some obsessive behavior and even got arrested twice after they got separated.

A year later Joan re-appeared, but this time claimed she was pregnant with his child. Charlie denied it, but Joan filled a paternity suit against him. Long story short, Joan had her child, they went to court and Charlie's lawyers tried to admit tests that proved he was not the father (blood test showing that the child's blood type was not possible if he was the father).

Unfortunately, at the time, California's courts didn't accept blood tests as evidence in legal trials. So they dismissed the tests and the judge ordered Charlie to pay child support for Joan's child until she turned 21! And he indeed paid for support until the child, Carol Ann, became 21 although it was widely known she was not his child.

The controversy around him increased after he announced he had married his newest romantic affair, young actress Oona O'Neill, some weeks after the paternity suit was filed. At the time he was 54 and Oona was 18. They remained married until his death, 18 years later, and after having 8 children!

ABRAHAM LINCOLN

He was a lawyer, a politician and the leader of the United States of America during the nation's greatest moral and political crisis, the Civil War. While alive, he abolished slavery, made the federal government stronger and modernized the economy. Unfortunately, he was assassinated. He was shot at the back of his head while attending a play. He died after being in a coma for 9 hours. His adventures though didn't end there.

After he was buried with honors, no significant security measures were put in place for guarding his tomb. And this seemed perfectly reasonable at the time; who would want to steal a dead president's body? The answer would be a small-time criminal boss called James "Big Jim" Kennally. His partner was in prison with a 10-year sentence and thought by stealing Lincoln's body and blackmailing the governor, he would get his partner back and make some ransom money.

It seemed like an easy job since there were no security measures at the grave. He assigned this job to 2 members of his gang. Those members had no body-snatching experience, so they hired a third person to help them out. What they thought was a professional "grave robber," was actually a professional informant of the Secret Service.

On the night of the job, the cemetery was filled with hidden Secret Service men who were waiting for the 3 man or the man's gang to steal the body. It was a total failure. The gang first didn't know how to pick the padlock of the tomb's chamber and they ended up cutting it with a file. After entering the tomb's chamber, they discovered the coffin was too heavy to move. They were considering their options when a hidden officer's pistol accidentally went off and they ran away. Obviously, they were arrested a couple of days later.

Although the body was never stolen, the custodians

of the grave were shocked some amateurs had come so close to stealing the body. They decided to secretly move the body themselves, without letting anyone know. The body was moved to the basement of the tomb's chamber in an unmarked grave. The body remained there until years later when proper security measures were installed onto the president's grave.

CHARLES DICKENS

He was one of the most important English writers and the greatest novelist of the Victorian era. He was an extremely pro-liferate writer and edited a weekly journal for 20 years. He wrote 15 novels and a lot of short stories and non-fiction articles. He even has an adjective named after him, "Dickensian," which is used to describe his style of writing. Charles though had a really tough time when he was young.

When he was 12 years old, his father that had accumulated a huge debt while living beyond his means. He was forced by his creditors into a debtor's prison in Southwark, London. The surprising fact is his wife and children joined him there, something that was quite common in Victorian England!

In a debtor's prison, you were supposed to work off your debt via labor. Charles, in order to help his financially troubled family, was forced to quit school and work 10-hour days at a warehouse pasting labels. These harsh working conditions made a strong impression on him and later influenced his writing style, most notably in his famous novel "Oliver Twist."

Although he had such a hard childhood, Charles as an adult turned out to be a more lighthearted guy, and most of his stories have happy endings.

JACK NICHOLSON

J ack is known for playing a wide range of roles, most commonly the anti-hero. At the time of this writing, he had 12 Oscar nominations, making him the most nominated male actor in the Academy's history. Although he is known mainly for his acting career, he has also worked as a director, producer, and screenwriter. The surprising story about his real parents though could easily be the plot of one of his movies.

Jack was a son of a showgirl named June Nicholson, and was born in 1937. She married a fellow showman named Donald in 1936, before learning he was already married! There were rumors Jack's real biological father might have been June's manager, Eddie. Nevertheless, that was not important at the time since June was only 17 years old, unmarried, with a child.

June's parents agreed to raise Jack as their own child, without revealing his true parentage and June, his real mother, would act as his sister. And this setup worked really well, until 1974 when Time magazine researchers learned and informed him about his true parents.

By the time he was informed about this, both his mother and grandmother were dead. Still, he mentioned that it was a really dramatic event learning about it, but it didn't traumatize him since he was already pretty well psychologically formed. When this was revealed, Jack was in the early days of his successful career and thankfully the reveal didn't seem to affect him much.

JULIUS CAESAR

The legendary Roman emperor was so great that his name became synonymous with the word "emperor." He is considered by many historians as the greatest military commander in history and extended the reach of the Roman Empire to Britain. Besides being a military general, he was also a politician and a historian. He played a critical role in the downfall of the Roman Republic and the rise of the Roman Empire. But he was not the humblest guy, not even when he was young.

When the emperor was young and traveling across

the Aegean Sea, he was taken hostage by pirates. The pirates, not knowing who he was, were discussing how much to ask for his release. They were thinking of asking for 20 talents (the ancient "currency"). When he heard them, he laughed aloud and arrogantly suggested them to ask for 50. That was a huge amount for the time and it took 38 days for Caesar's men to gather and deliver the ransom amount.

During his captivity time, the future emperor was relaxed and joined them in most of their everyday activities, ignoring the fact they were his capturers. He was acting more like these men were his royal bodyguards. He was also working on his poems and speeches and reading them out loud. When some of the pirates didn't admire his work, he would call them barbarians and threatened jokingly, to hang them all. When he was going for sleep he would order them to keep quiet.

The pirates were amused by his behavior thinking that he was just young and not realizing the seriousness of the situation. After they received the enormous payment, the pirates kept their word and released the young Julius.

But the story didn't end there. Caesar gathered a naval force and went back to the island where he had been captured. The pirates were still there and he captured them and put them into a local prison. The governor of Asia was delaying to punish (i.e. execute) them, probably longing for their money.

So he personally took the issue into his own hands.

He went to their prison, got them out, and had them crucified like he had joking about doing when he was a hostage. As a sign of mercy, he first cut their throat, probably so they wouldn't suffer a slow death. It's quite clear Julius was ruthless from a young age and probably no one would mess with him (except when he was assassinated).

PUYI

The last emperor of China, Puyi or Pu-yi, had a really turbulent life. He was appointed emperor of China when he was 2 years old, emperor of Manchukuo (a Japanese puppet state that lasted for around 10 years) and then imprisoned when the People's Republic of China was established. Nevertheless, he had his fun times when he was a young boy.

One of his tutors told Puyi about the relatively new invention at the time, the telephone. Young Puyi really wanted one to be installed in the palace. But his advisors told him it would be against their traditions to do such a thing. The boy insisted, and his advisors had his father tell him it wouldn't be wise to give the ability to outsiders to call into the palace. Probably the real reason they didn't want him to have a telephone was their belief that once having made contact with the outside world, it would be very difficult to restrain the young emperor within the palace.

Long story short, Puyi finally got his phone. And he really did made contact with the outside world in the form of prank calls from the Beijing telephone directory, like ordering large meals to random addresses and calling famous opera singers.

PYTHAGORAS

The great ancient Greek philosopher, also known as Pythagoras of Samos, has influenced through his political and religious teachings the entire Western philosophy. Whatever knowledge we have about him is mainly from third parties, but we are almost certain he traveled to Croton (today located in Italy) and founded a school. Students there were sworn to secrecy and lived an ascetic life. It was a kind of cult with their own beliefs, life theories, and diet (most probably some form of vegetarianism).

Pythagoras was active in various fields such as ethics, mathematics, metaphysics, music, mysticism, politics and religion. But maybe the most famous of Pythagoras' teachings is the concept of metempsychosis, which means that every soul is immortal and upon the body's death it enters into a new body.

He also had a strange dietary rule that it was forbidden to eat beans. We don't know for sure, but it is believed this was due to his theory that every time a human passed gas a part of their soul was lost. Therefore, he developed a strong belief that beans had to be avoided at all costs.

Fast forward to his death, which we are again not sure how it happened. But multiple sources claim Pythagoras made enemies from his political endeavors. At some point when they were chasing him to kill him, he stumbled upon a bean field. He stood still, not sure what to do. This hesitation turned out to be deadly. His enemies caught up with him and took his life.

NAPOLÉON BONAPARTE

The French general is considered one of the greatest commanders in history. His strategies and campaigns are still studied in military schools all around the globe. Napoleon was born in Corsica and his family had an Italian origin. He was an artillery officer when the French Revolution started and he took advantage of the opportunities presented to him to rise rapidly to the rank of general at the age of 24! He went on to conquer almost the entire continental Europe. His most famous, and final, defeat was the battle of Waterloo, after which he was exiled by the British to the remote island of Saint Helena in the middle of the Atlantic ocean. Napoleon though had another defeat that is not that well known.

In the summer of 1807, he had just signed the Treaties of Tilsit, which was really favorable to him. Napoleon decided to celebrate the big victory with a rabbit hunt, which I guess was fun at the time. Therefore, he assigned his chief of staff to organize it and invite the most prominent men in the military. We are not sure of the exact number of rabbits that were collected, but some sources say up to a thousand of them!

It was expected that as soon as they were released they would eagerly flee. Unfortunately, the exact opposite happened. Instead of running away the bunnies headed towards the general. The bunny horde reached him and started climbing up the general's legs. Panicked, Napoleon's men were trying to beat them off with sticks, but there was just too many of them. He managed to escape after all by fleeing to his private coach.

The most probable explanation is that it was his chief of staff's fault. Instead of collecting wild rapids, he purchased tame rabbits that were used to being around people. When they were released, they were expecting Napoleon to feed them rather than to shoot them!

SYLVESTER STALLONE

The Hollywood star famous for the Rocky and Rambo movie series, among others, had experienced difficult times before becoming a star. Michael Sylvester Gardenzio Stallone, as his real name is, has an Italian father and an American mother of French and Ukrainian-Jewish descent. While trying to make it in the film industry he even had to star in a softcore pornographic movie to pay rent after finding himself homeless for several days! But this was not the only sacrifice he made to stay afloat until he could make it big.

According to a rumor many considered a stunt by his publicists, but later was confirmed to be true in interviews, right before writing and selling the script for the first Rocky movie, Stallone was struggling financially. He was in such a bad situation financially that he slept in the New York bus station for 3 days.

Unable to find another source of income, he tried to sell his dog for $100. He actually sold it for $50. A few weeks later he sold the Rocky's script, for a handsome amount, and tried to buy the dog back. The new owner though was not willing to sell back the dog. Although it was only a few weeks since he had the dog, he claimed his kids loved it and he didn't want to sell it.

He was finally convinced to sell the dog for $3,000 and a small part in the movie. Both the ex-owner, Little Jimmy, and the bullmastiff dog, Butkus, appeared in the first Rocky movie.

AESCHYLUS

Aeschylus was not just an ancient Greek playwright; he was the father of tragedy (the theatrical genre). The knowledge of the entire genre begins with his work. It's sad that only seven out of the estimated seventy to ninety (!) plays he wrote have survived. One of his most important contributions was the presentation of his plays as trilogies, something that survives until this day.

Anthony Grin

At some point in his life, Aeschylus received a prophecy that he would die from a falling object. He was a great soldier and he survived many battles. Since then he was avoiding staying indoors to avoid the prophecy. While visiting Sicily from Athens, for one last time, he was killed by a tortoise that was dropped by an eagle. It seems that in the area there is a type of eagle which feeds on tortoises by dropping them onto hard objects, such as rocks. Most probably, the bird confused his bald head for a rock, suitable for opening the turtle that it was holding.

That was a tragic ending for the father of tragedy. But take all of these with a grain of salt since the story might have been just a misunderstanding of the iconography of his gravestone.

www.ingramcontent.com/pod-product-compliance
Lightning Source LLC
Chambersburg PA
CBHW020332290526
45785CB00007B/3033